The Anatomy of a Writing Tutoring Session: A Handbook to Establishing a Foundation of Success for Both Writer and Tutor

Chloe Crull

D0557235

Contents

Acknowledgments

Thank you to the Clovis Community College Tutorial Center for privileging me with a foundation of writing tutoring knowledge.

Thank you to the University of California: Berkeley Student Learning Center Writing Program for guiding me to expand and sharpen my engagement with writing tutor pedagogy.

Thank you to the writers who have provided me feedback throughout my years of tutoring.

Thank you to the tutors who have worked and grown alongside me.

Thank you to the professors who have provided me with opportunities to take on the role of both student and educator in their classrooms.

Author's Note

Thank you for reading this guide to conducting a writing tutoring session. I like to think of tutors as professional question-askers, and I intend this guide to serve as a way for my fellow tutors to visualize the tutoring process as a conversation and learn to establish the foundation for a professional and effective tutoring session.

The Anatomy of a Writing Tutoring Session

The tutoring session involves five steps:

1. Building rapport
2. Establishing an agenda
3. Guiding the conversation
4. Wrapping up and reflecting
5. Receiving and analyzing feedback

Throughout the conversation, the writer establishes the agenda and provides the content knowledge for the discussion. The tutor sets boundaries and adheres to the policies of the tutoring center while providing insightful observations, asking stimulating questions, and introducing strategies to help the writer engage their[1] critical thinking and develop their writing skills and process.

---

[1] I use the pronoun "their" for singular nouns to remain gender inclusive.

Building Rapport

In order to establish a foundation for both writer and tutor to have a successful session, the tutor must first take the time to build rapport with the writer. Whether the session is thirty minutes or an hour, it is critical for the tutor to spend the first few minutes to introduce themself and make the writer feel welcomed into the center and engaged with the tutor. In this sense, the tutor should initially approach the writer as a person, not a tutee. When conversing, the tutor should encourage an empowering mindset that shifts the writer away from negative thinking. To build rapport with a writer, the tutor may consider these steps:

1. Introduce yourself by offering your name and pronouns. Ask for the writer's name.

> **Tutor**: Hello! Welcome to the Writing Center. My name is Chloe, I use she/her pronouns,

and I'll be your writing tutor today. What's your name?

Writer: Hello. My name is Mitchell, and I use he/him pronouns.

2. Pronouncing the writer's name correctly in response, inquire about the writer's well-being in the semester thus far.

Tutor: It's lovely to meet you, Mitchell. How have you been enjoying the semester so far?

Writer: Thanks. It's fine, I guess.

Tutor: That's good. Is this your first time taking college classes?

Writer: No, I'm a second-year student.

Tutor: Nice. I'm a fourth-year English major with a minor in Education. What's your major?

Writer: Cool. I'm a Sociology major.

> **Tutor**: Wow! That's really neat. <u>Are your classes related to your academic or personal interests?</u>
>
> **Writer**: Not really. To be honest, this class is really stressing me out right now. It suddenly piled up on me out of nowhere, and I have so much work to do.

3. Acknowledge the writer's response. Inquire if the writer has utilized tutoring services before and provide a brief overview of the tutoring session. The overview should address the time restraints of the conversation, encourage the writer to take notes or add comments to their document, mention a wrap-up and reflection in the last five minutes of the session, mention a feedback form, and invite the writer to ask questions about the structure of the session.

> **Tutor:** I understand that. I have been really stressed out by my Linguistics class this week. It's a great choice to utilize your resources

and reach out to tutoring services, though. <u>Is this your first time visiting the Writing Center?</u>

Writer: Yeah, I haven't been here before.

Tutor: No worries, Mitchell! I'm excited to welcome you into the Writing Center and introduce you to our tutoring services. <u>Today's conversation will be fifty minutes, so we will have until about 4:00 for this session.</u> We'll focus on any aspects of writing that you would like to discuss. As we establish an agenda for our session, please keep in mind that a follow-up session may be necessary if we are not able to cover everything today. <u>During our conversation, please take notes or add comments to your document as we read and discuss.</u> <u>In the last five minutes of the session, we'll wrap up and reflect, so that will be around 3:55.</u> This will give us an opportunity to review what we discussed and think about your next steps as a writer. <u>After our wrap-up and reflection, I will provide an anonymous feedback form.</u> The Writing Center asks all writers who utilize the tutoring services to complete this form after each session to ensure the highest-quality service for our writers. <u>Do you have any questions about our tutoring session today?</u>

Establishing an Agenda

After building rapport with the writer, the tutor should allow the writer to establish a meaningful agenda. A meaningful agenda allows the writer to realistically address their concerns in alignment with their goals and ultimately leave the center with strategies to further develop their writing process. While establishing the agenda, the tutor should help the writer modify the agenda as needed for time management, but the writer should remain in control of the agenda so that they maintain ownership of their writing voice and process.

1. Answer any questions the writer asks about the session overview. Inquire about the course that brings the writer into the center. Reference appointment notes if available so that the tutor is prepared and respects the time that the writer takes to fill out the tutoring form.

Tutor: Now that we've had a brief overview of how our session is going to look, I would love to hear more about the class that brings you to the Writing Center. In your appointment notes, you mentioned that you're here for Women and Gender Studies 126. Would you mind telling me a bit more about the main topics of the course and the types of concepts you have been discussing in class?

Writer: Sure. So, we've been talking about American women's role during the Civil War because most people focus on the men who were soldiers, but the women actually did a lot. When the soldiers went to war, the wives suddenly had to run their husband's businesses, and they had to volunteer to provide rations and supplies to soldiers. They still had to provide for themselves and their children on top of all of that.

2. Acknowledge the writer's response. Inquire about the writer's feelings toward the course.

> **Tutor**: Wow, that's a really interesting point. It sounds like there is a lot to unpack in the course. <u>Have you been enjoying the class and its content so far?</u>
>
> **Writer**: I guess. It's just a lot of reading, and I feel like I fall behind, so I'm not as interested because I don't know as much. I don't like participating if I don't think that I can keep up.

3. Acknowledge and validate the writer's feelings while continuing to encourage an empowering mindset that shifts the writer away from negative thinking, especially if they feel stressed about the course or frustrated by the professor's expectations. Ask about the types of assignments and discussions the writer has experienced in class.

> **Tutor**: That's totally understandable. Since I'm an English major, my classes require me to read a lot, and there have definitely been times where I have fallen behind. You've already made a great decision to utilize your resources and reach out to the Writing Cen-

ter for help, so that's a great start. I've also found that asking my professors for deadline extensions can help when I'm feeling overwhelmed. <u>What kinds of assignments have you been completing in class so far?</u>

Writer: Thanks. That's a good point. I might ask for an extension on the essay we just got assigned. We've been doing a lot of discussion board posts and summary-response assignments, but this essay is killer.

4. Shift the conversation to the specific assignment that prompted the writer to seek tutoring services.

Tutor: Yeah, I understand. <u>Is the essay the assignment that brings you to the Writing Center?</u>

Writer: Yeah, it's really stressing me out. I haven't written anything this long in forever, and it was really hard.

5. Request to see the prompt and rubric. Ask for the writer's understanding of the prompt.

> **Tutor**: I get that. It can be really daunting to even begin an essay, so I'm proud of you for sticking with it. It would be really helpful to review the prompt for more context about the essay. <u>Can you walk me through the prompt and explain to me how you understood the assignment?</u> Also, if there's a rubric for the assignment, we can look at that, too.
>
> **Writer**: Sure. Let me grab it . . . It's kind of short. It just asks us to argue whether or not we think the Union would have won the war without the support of women aiding in the war effort. It also says, "Cite four scholarly, peer-reviewed sources to support your argument."

6. Inquire where the writer is in the writing process.[2]

---

[2] Tutors should not assume that the writer already has a draft prepared. By inviting the writer to seek tutoring at any stage of the writing process, the writer understands that writing involves more than drafting and editing, and the writer is able to develop their own writing process.

Tutor: Okay, thank you. So, it sounds like you're creating an original argument about women's contributions to the success of the Union, and you need sources to support the argument. <u>Where are you in the writing process for this assignment?</u>

Writer: Right. I already have a full draft, but it just feels really messy. I have two more days to finish it, but it just feels like a lot of work.

7. Inquire about the writer's goals and repeat their goals in acknowledgement.

Tutor: I would love to hear more about your goals so that we can establish a meaningful agenda for our time together. In your appointment notes, you mentioned that you wanted to improve the structure of an essay. <u>Would you mind telling me more about what you mean by structure?</u>

Writer: Yeah, sure. I feel like my argument goes in different directions and gets shaky.

8. Once the writer elaborates their goals, ask how the writer plans to utilize the tutoring session. Although similar to step 7, this step allows the writer to visualize how they plan to achieve their goals with the help of a tutor. It pushes the writer to shift beyond static goals such as wanting to "improve their structure" and encourages them to begin thinking about the conversations they will engage in to help them achieve their goals.

> **Tutor**: Okay. Thank you for giving me more context about that. <u>Thinking about structure as a goal, what would you like to get out of our tutoring session today?</u>
>
> **Writer**: Umm, I don't know. I guess I would like help finding where my paper falls apart and figure out how to fix it. I just don't really know where to begin is the thing.

9. Meet the writer where they are in the writing process. If the writer is in the revision stage, for example, request to review the draft.

Tutor: That's okay. We'll get through it together. <u>Do you have your draft with you?</u>

Writer: Yeah.

Tutor: Great. <u>Would you feel comfortable reading it out loud while I follow along on the paper?</u> As you read, we'll make sure to keep your goals of structure in mind.

Writer: Yeah, sure.

Guiding the Conversation

Throughout the tutoring session, the tutor should encourage the writer to find power in their academic voice. The writer should control the conversation and contribute most of the dialogue. The tutor should provide a balance of critical questions and insightful observations that help the writer develop their critical thinking and writing skills through the creation of knowledge as opposed to the recollection of information.[3] Throughout the session, the tutor should embody a "guide on the side" and allow the writer to act as the "sage on the stage."[4] While guiding the conversation, the tutor should employ the following strategies:

---

[3] Tofade, Toyin et al. "Best Practice Strategies for Effective Use of Questions as a Teaching Tool." *American Journal of Pharmaceutical Education*, vol. 77, no. 7, 2013: 155. doi:10.5688/ajpe777155

[4] King, Alison. "From Sage on the Stage to Guide on the Side." College Teaching, vol. 41, no. 1, 1993, pp. 30–35. JSTOR, www.jstor.org/stable/27558571. Accessed 28 July 2021.

Use a variety of interrogative words such as who, what, where, why, and when to generate different avenues of thought:

What is your thesis statement?

How does this sentence represent your thesis statement?

Why does this sentence represent your thesis statement?

In the above example, the "**What**" question enables the writer to answer with a simple "This sentence is my thesis statement." On the other hand, the "**How**" and "**Why**" questions require the writer to provide more context about their thesis and defend both its structure and logic.

While the writer reads their drafts, take notes considering your experience as a reader.

What questions arise as the writer reads? What ideas do you wish the writer expanded?

"As a reader, I found myself asking: 'What is balanced focalization?' I'm not familiar with that term, so I was confused when you started using it."

"To be honest, I'm a little confused in this section. I see that you start off talking about suffrage up here, but then you talk about women running the businesses down here in the same paragraph. How do you think these ideas connect?"

Refer to the writer's goals throughout the conversation:

"How do you feel this strategy can help you achieve your goal of improving structure?"

"Where can you apply this idea to your original goal of improving the structure of your paper?"

Check in with the writer:

"I just want to **pause** here and check in with you. How do you feel about our conversation and these strategies thus far?"

"We've been talking for a few minutes now, so how would you feel about pausing to write down some of your ideas?"

Use positive language:

"You shouldn't use a quote there."

vs

"I think moving this quote to your body paragraphs would help to better support your ideas and make the introduction less overwhelming for the reader."

Provide specific feedback:

"It looks fine."

vs

"I really like how you use your source here. It supports your ideas and address-es the counterargument."

"This is confusing."

vs

"I think your structure would benefit from a topic sentence that introduces your idea. I find myself confused when you jump straight into the quotation here."

Strategies to Share with Writers to Develop their Writing Process

Throughout the tutoring session, the tutor should provide the writer with strategies to develop their writing process. The introduction of these writing strategies embodies the ancient proverb, "If you give a man a fish, you feed him for a day. If you teach him how to fish, you feed him for a lifetime." By equipping writers with strategies, tutors help writers develop their writing processes and empower writers to engage with different elements of the writing process without feeling the need for a tutor's presence to produce "good writing."

Reading Strategy 1: Annotate Texts with Questions, Comments, and Doodles

As writers read texts, writers can take notes directly on the texts as a form of notetaking called annotating. While annotating, writers should aim to critically analyze texts through their annotations rather than recycling information.[5] Instead of merely highlighting or underlining words, writers can write clarifying statements for difficult passages, ask questions prompted by the reading, and doodle images or emojis that represent the writer's reactions or connections to the text. By annotating, writers can visualize the text as a conversation with the author and enhance their engagement with the material. Additionally, annotations allow for easier recollection of the text since writers can review the notes generated through annotating instead of rereading the entire document.

Reading Strategy 2: Annotate Texts with Alternating Colors Each Read

While reading a text, writers can annotate their texts with different colors each time they

---

[5] Liu, Keming. "Annotation as an Index to Critical Writing." *Urban Education*, vol. 41, no. 2, Mar. 2006, pp. 192–207. *Academic Search Complete*, doi:10.1177/0042085905282261.

read the text. So, the first time a writer reads a text, they can annotate notes in blue. The second time that writer reads the text, they can annotate notes in purple. The third time that writer reads the text, they can annotate notes in green. This allows writers to visualize how their thought processes change and new insights develop from each engagement with the text.

Reading Strategy 3: Carry Copies of Difficult Passages

Encourage writers to carry a copy of difficult passages with them throughout the day. If writers have a challenging reading assignment or a difficult poem to digest, they should carry a copy of the text (or a section of the text) in their pocket or on their phones. When writers find a few minutes of free time standing in line or waiting for class to begin, they can read the copy and allow their brains to simultaneously dissect small sections of the text and incubate the ideas between each reading. Additionally, rereading allows writers to articulate connections between main ideas, supporting details, and text organization.[6]

Brainstorming Strategy 1: Cluster diagram

The "cluster diagram" refers to a brainstorming strategy where a writer connects ideas together on a visual web. To begin, the writer should write a word or phrase that describes their initial idea and circle the word or phrase. Next, writers should add branches to the main circle, adding details as necessary and continuing to expand and group ideas with circles and branches. Consider this cluster diagram used to brainstorm ideas for a persuasive essay about women's contributions to the Civil War:

---

[6] Hedin, Laura R., and Greg Conderman. "Teaching Students to Comprehend Informational Text Through Rereading." *Reading Teacher*, vol. 63, no. 7, Apr. 2010, pp. 556–565. *Academic Search Complete*, doi:10.1598/RT.63.7.3.

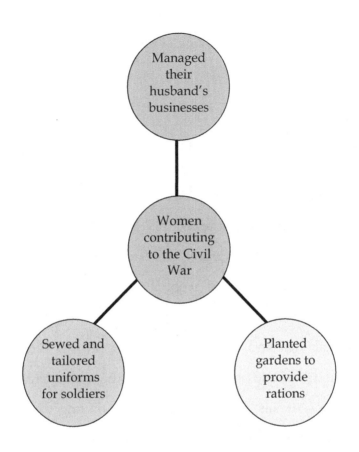

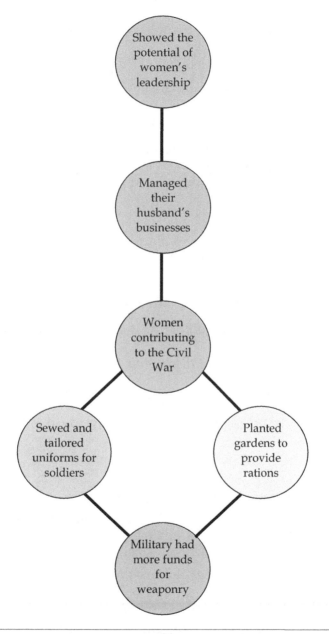

Showed the potential of women's leadership

Managed their husband's businesses

Women contributing to the Civil War

Sewed and tailored uniforms for soldiers

Planted gardens to provide rations

Military had more funds for weaponry

Brainstorming Strategy 2: Freewriting

Freewriting allows writers to "braindump" their ideas onto paper. Writers may set an alarm for two minutes and write as much as they can about their topic. If they find themselves running out of ideas before the two minutes finishes, writers can engage in meta-freewriting, which involves the writer thinking about *why* they're writing and how the writing project could influence themselves or others. Tutors may consider engaging in the freewriting activity with the writer so that the writer and tutor can discuss each other's ideas and thought processes. Consider this example freewrite about women's contributions to the Civil War:

Women contributed a lot more to the Civil War than most people realize. Most people focus on the contributions of men because they represented the soldier population, so a lot of women's efforts go unrecognized. For example, a lot of people don't know that women had to run their husbands' businesses once the husbands left to fight in the war. This was a huge responsibility for these women. Also, not only did the women's professional lives change, but their personal lives as well. Their previous leisure time was suddenly dedicated to sewing uniforms for soldiers or planting gardens to provide rations. I want to write about women's contributions to the Civil War because it is important to listen to the voices unrecognized by history. I also think it ties really interestingly into the advocation for women's rights because women defended our country just like men did, so women deserve the social and political influence that men have. This reminds me that I also want to tie the history of women's efforts in the Civil War to the lack of representation for women in politics . . .

Brainstorming Strategy 3: Incubate Ideas

If time allows, encourage writers to take breaks from their writing and "sleep on" their ideas. If a writer receives a prompt for an essay, encourage them to read the prompt immediately, freewrite for two minutes, and allow their ideas to incubate. These periods of incubation promote critical thinking and creative problem-solving.[7] Writers should especially incubate their ideas overnight by reading their notes immediately before bedtime, as opposed to after a day of wakefulness, because sleep stabilizes declarative memory and enhances memory retention.[8]

Thesis-Building Strategy 1: Begin with a Research Question

When drafting an essay, encourage students to begin with a research question, not a thesis statement. By starting with a research question, writers can research and investigate a conundrum

---

[7] Ritter, Simone M, and Ap Dijksterhuis. "Creativity—The Unconscious Foundations of the Incubation Period." *Frontiers in Human Neuroscience,* vol. 8, 15. 11 Apr. 2014, doi:10.3389/fnhum.2014.00215

[8] Payne, Jessica D et al. "Memory for Semantically Related and Unrelated Declarative Information: The Benefit of Sleep, The Cost of Wake." *PloS one* vol. 7,3 (2012): e33079. doi:10.1371/journal.pone.0033079

---

that interests them before worrying about creating a solidified, structured claim. Besides, writing is a recursive process that requires rereading texts and revising drafts. Thus, the thesis statement should result from deliberate engagement with texts and ideas rather than the writer's first reaction to the prompt.[9] As writers investigate their research question, they constantly develop and revise their working thesis.

Thesis-Building Strategy 2: Consider the Audience

When writers formulate ideas, they should consider the intended audience to ensure they deliver the message in the most effective medium to generate its intended effect. For example, consider a writer drafting an essay to persuade a local school in Los Angeles to build streetlights around

---

[9] Student Learning Center Writing Program. *Thesis Statements*. Spring 2020. *Google Docs* file.

the campus to increase the safety of children walking to school. Instead of directing the essay to concerned parents of students attending the school, the writer should direct the essay to Los Angeles County because the county officials possess the ability to generate the change desired by the writer. So, the writer must consider the most effective method of communicating with the most relevant audience.

Thesis-Building Strategy 3: Consider "What the Paper is About" vs "What the Paper will Do"

When writers think of a prompt, they envision a piece of paper that tells them "what their essay should be about." However, writers can better envision their ideas when they think of a prompt as a piece of paper that tells them "what their essay should *do.*" This also helps writers from trapping themselves in informative circles of only providing summarized information rather than creating original arguments. Additionally, this encourages writers to approach writing as a tool for sharing one's voice and generating social change.

Thesis-Building Strategy 4: The Main Claim, the How Factor, and the So What Factor

When drafting a thesis statement, encourage writers to consider three critical factors: the main claim, the "how" factor, and the "so what" factor. The main claim asserts the argument, the "how" factor explains how the argument manifests, and the "so what" factor emphasizes the significance of the argument and indicates why the audience should care about the argument.

Example: Although American K-12 curriculum emphasizes the heroic efforts of men during the Civil War, schools should teach students about the contributions of women by educating students about the responsibilities women undertook in the absences of their husbands because the lack of historical accreditation for women translates to a contemporary lack of representation for women in political spheres.

Drafting Strategy 1: Use Prompts as an Outline

Since prompts provide the instructions necessary to complete an assignment, writers can convert prompts into outlines of the information required in their papers. First, writers copy and paste the prompt into a document and add spaces between the different sections of the prompt. These spaces provide room for writers to brainstorm bullet-point notes for each section of the prompt.

Example prompt: Consider how American K-12 curriculum portrays the contributions of women during the Civil War. In a 1,500-word essay, argue whether the efforts of women have been accurately represented in curriculum. How did women contribute to the war effort, and how do schools portray these contributions? Whose perspectives are highlighted by the curriculum, and how does this affect the portrayal of women during the Civil War? What are the social and political ramifications of this representation? Cite four scholarly, peer-reviewed sources to support your argument.

Prompt Converted to Outline:

In a 1,500-word essay, consider how American K-12 curriculum portrays the contributions of women during the Civil War and argue whether the efforts of women have been accurately represented in curriculum.

How did women contribute to the war effort,
- o sewed uniforms for soldiers
- o planted gardens to grow crops to provide rations for soldiers
- o managed their husbands' businesses while they served in the

war

and how do schools portray these contributions?
- o journal entries from historical figures in history

Whose perspectives are highlighted by the curriculum,
- students study texts written from the perspective of straight white men rather than exploring the perspectives of all people involved in the Civil War, such as women and other minority groups
    - ▪ so, schools should require a more diverse selection of texts

and how does this affect the portrayal of women during the Civil War?
- o women's voices and contributions are underrepresented
    - people don't think of women as offering as much significance to history as men

What are the social and political ramifications of this representation?

- social ramifications = women considered inferior and dismissed in social circles
- political ramifications = women considered less influential than men and incapable of leadership
  - lack of representation for women as less women fill political positions

Cite four scholarly, peer-reviewed sources to support your argument.
- "Civil Women" article by Vladimay Kenskov talks about women managing businesses
- *Home Base* documentary by Resna Bevee talks about women growing gardens for rations
- "Sewing Civil Souls" poem by Iliad Mendal talks about women enduring hardships and balancing domestic responsibilities while trying to contribute to the war
- Review class readings to find counterarguments to address for fourth source

Drafting Strategy 2: Use Text-to-Speech to Put Pen to Paper

When writers encounter writer's block or become "self-censoring writers" by refusing to write less-than-perfect sentences,[10] writers may consider utilizing speech-to-text features on computers or smartphones. For example, individuals can access Microsoft Word on their phone or computer and use the "Dictate" feature to activate their microphone. Afterward, the individual can verbally speak through their ideas aloud, allowing their thoughts to freely flow onto the Word document as the program converts the speech to written text.

[10] Meyer, Emily, and Louise Smith. "Promoting Fluency I: Getting Started." The Practical Tutor. Oxford University Press, 1987. pp. 43-66.

Drafting Strategy 3: Start with the Body Paragraphs

Writers may feel intimidated by the need for an introduction and thesis statement, so encourage writers to draft their body paragraphs first. Drafting the body paragraphs allows writers to engage with their thoughts and *think through* their ideas before connecting them into an original, cohesive argument. This strategy also allows writers to avoid the task of introducing an argument they have not yet developed.

Drafting Strategy 4: Consider Previous Experiences with Writing Assignments

When encountering a new writing assignment, writers can reflect on their previous experiences with similar assignments to devise a more efficient strategy for completing the assignment. Tutors can encourage writers to pause and reflect on similar assignments they completed in the past.

What strategies made the process easier? What made the process more stressful or confusing? This practice of metacognition allows writers to visualize more beneficial approaches to the writing process and improves the quality of writing by fostering positive attitudes towards writing and enhancing writers' capacities for higher-order thinking.[11]

Citing Sources Strategy 1: The 3-part Citation

"The 3-part citation" refers to citing sources using a signal phrase, in-text citation, and corresponding reference entry for each source. The signal phrase introduces the author of the source and provides credentials if necessary to clarify the credibility and relevancy of the source. Depending on the citation style, the in-text cita-

[11] Cer, Erkan. "The Instruction of Writing Strategies: The Effect of the Metacognitive Strategy on the Writing Skills of Pupils in Secondary Education." *SAGE Open*, Apr. 2019, doi:10.1177/2158244019842681.

tion provides minimal citation information about the author, page number, and year of the source. The corresponding reference entry, commonly referred to as a "Works Cited" or "References" page, provides the full citation entry for the source, including the name of the author and publication information about the text.

Example: Lilac Sinclair, a Professor of Gender Studies at Venemoth University, states, "Women not only had to raise children and worry about their husbands, but they suddenly had to learn skills like accounting, record-keeping, and staff management" (17).

Works Cited

Sinclair, Lilac. "Civil War Women and Suffrage." *Civilian Women in the Civil War,* vol. 17, no. 1, 2017, pp. 3-78.

Citing Sources Strategy 2: Quote Sandwich

The "quote sandwich" refers to sandwiching a citation between an author's original thoughts. This technique coaxes authors into properly introducing and analyzing the citations that they use, therefore ensuring that they apply their research as opposed to merely dropping it into the text.

Example: In addition to sewing uniforms and growing victory gardens, women also contributed to the war effort by managing their husbands' businesses in their absences. Since many men had to leave their families to serve in the war, their wives had to take over the businesses to avoid closure and bankruptcy. According to Lilac Sinclair, a Professor of Gender Studies at Venemoth University, "Women not only had to raise children and worry about their husbands, but they suddenly had to learn skills like accounting, record-keeping, and staff management" (17). Given the sudden surge of women in business sectors, women proved their significance by maintaining both domestic and economic foundations of the nation, thus establishing themselves as capable influencers of society. As a result of these contributions, more men and women began advocating for women's suffrage so that women could extend their social and economic influences to the political sphere.

Revising Strategy 1: Reading Drafts Aloud

Reading aloud enables writers to hear their writing as spoken communication. Since all writing is a form of communication, aligning the written clarity and spoken clarity of a message increases the likelihood that the audience will receive the message intended by the author. "Good writers" are usually "good readers," and "good readers" possess strong comprehension skills.

In order to develop reading comprehension, writers must first develop listening comprehension.[12] By reading their work aloud, writers gain a better understanding of their language and how to restructure their sentences to best communicate their intended message. Additionally, reading aloud may help writers identify areas where they should double check their grammar. Although not every natural pause or stumble signal a punctuation rule, reading aloud texts allows writers to identify rough sentences that may require structural smoothing.

Revising Strategy 2: Reverse Outline

The "reverse outline" refers to an outline of an essay draft used for revising rather than prewriting. Unlike a traditional outline, a reverse outline is created after a draft is completed. By creating a reverse outline, writers work backwards and dissect the main idea of each paragraph they

---

[12] Hogan, Tiffany P., et al. "On the Importance of Listening Comprehension." *International Journal of Speech-Language Pathology*, vol. 16, 3, 2014: 199-207. doi:10.3109/17549507.2014.904441

have written as they appear in order. Typically, writers summarize the main idea of each paragraph into one sentence, which allows writers to visualize the progression of their ideas by stripping away the extra details and information around the main ideas.

Revising Strategy 3: Color-Coding Key Elements of Paragraphs

The "color-coding" strategy refers to color-coding key elements of each paragraph to ensure consistent, logical structure. Color-coding allows writers to visualize the structure of their paragraphs and identify inconsistencies. For example, writers may choose to color topic sentences as green, citations as red, citation analysis and commentary as blue, and concluding sentences as purple. If a writer notices a paragraph is primarily red, then that may indicate that the writer should return to the paragraph and minimize the citations to illuminate more of their own ideas. If a writer notices that some of their paragraphs lack green, then that may indicate that the writer is diving into details without introducing the topic of the paragraph.

Topic sentences establish the main point of the paragraph. Citations allow writers to support their ideas or address counterarguments with sources. Citation analysis and commentary allow writers to respond to and apply their sources. Concluding sentences wrap up the paragraph and connect its main idea to the overall thesis of the paper.

Revising Strategy 4: Emphasize Higher Order Concerns Over Lower Order Concerns

Encourage writers to emphasize Higher Order Concerns like logic and structure over

Lower Order Concerns like grammar.[13] Although writers and tutors may engage in conversations about grammar, tutors should encourage writers to improve their argument before improving their grammar. Grammatical errors only raise concerns in tutoring sessions if the grammatical errors inhibit the clarity of the writer's message, and writers will not help themselves by grammatically perfecting a sentence that contains a weak structure or poor use of logic.

Revising Strategy 5: Isolate and Compare Topic Sentences with the Thesis Statement

Encourage writers to copy each topic sentence and paste them together in a document. Writers should also paste their thesis statement above the topic sentences. This strategy allows

---

[13] "Higher Order Concerns (HOCs) and Lower Order Concerns (LOCs)." *Purdue Online Writing Lab*, 2021,
https://owl.purdue.edu/owl/research_and_citation/mla_style/mla_format ting_and_style_guide/mla_works_cited_electronic_sources.html

writers to compare their main ideas and identify instances of repetition. Additionally, this strategy allows writers to consider the organization of ideas and ensure that their main ideas support the thesis statement.

Time Management Strategy 1: Divide Workloads by Word Counts and Page Numbers

Once writers receive reading and writing assignments, encourage them to divide their workload so that they read a certain number of pages per day and write a certain number of words per day. By using this strategy, writers complete a small amount of work each day and establish a much more manageable workload.

Example: A writer has 9 days to finish reading 45 pages of a book for one class and write a 1,500-word essay for another class. Saving 1 day to reserve time for revision and unexpected delays, the writer should divide the number of pages and number of words by the 8 remaining days:

45 pages ÷ 8 days ≈ 5.5 pages to read per day

1,500 words ÷ 8 days ≈ 187 words to write

per day

If the student follows this schedule, they will finish reading and writing with an entire day left to review and revise.

Time Management Strategy 2: Pomodoro Technique

Invented by Francesco Cirillo in the 1980s, the Pomodoro Technique involves alternating between time increments of completing work and taking breaks.[14] For example, a writer facing a difficult assignment can dedicate fifteen minutes to the assignment, take a five-minute break without socializing or using digital devices, dedicate anoth-

---

[14] "The Pomodoro Technique." *Francesco Cirillo, Cirillo Consulting GMBH*, Berlin, https://francescocirillo.com/pages/pomodoro-technique

er fifteen minutes to the assignment, take another five-minute break without socializing or using digital devices, and repeat the process. Writers can adjust the amount of time dedicated to completing work and taking breaks to construct the most appropriate schedule. Additionally, writers can utilize the Pomodoro Technique in combination with Time Management Strategy 1 to divide workloads and complete smaller amounts of work over increments of time.

Wrapping Up and Reflecting

1. Provide a time warning *before* the wrap-up to allow writers to ask their final question(s) but remain firm about time restraints.

> **Tutor**: It looks like we have about ten minutes left in our session. Are there any pressing questions you would like to conclude with? We can then reserve the last five minutes to wrap up, reflect, and plan ahead.
>
> **Writer**: Okay. Yeah, I wanted to ask one more question about citations.
>
> **Tutor**: Sure thing. We will try our best to answer your final question about citations in its entirety, but please note that we may need to schedule another session if we don't fully answer your question before we reflect on our session and plan your next steps.

2. Ask the writer to reflect on the tutoring session. Make sure that the writer reiterates the specific elements and strategies that aided them in devel-

oping their writing process.

Tutor: Alright. So, when we first started talking, you mentioned that you wanted to review your structure because you felt like your paper was falling apart towards the conclusion. <u>How do you feel about the structure of your paper now?</u>

Writer: I feel better. It flows a lot nicer, and it makes a lot more sense now. I also think my argument is stronger, too, because it sounds more put-together.

Tutor: That's great! <u>How do you feel your writing process has been impacted by this session?</u>

Writer: Umm, I guess I know how to keep the focus in my paper better.

Tutor: I'm happy to hear that. <u>What specific strategies stood out to you in the session?</u>

Writer: The reverse outline really helped. I never thought about outlining my own essay before. So, I feel more confident about using that.

3. Inquire about the writer's next steps and ask if the writer feels confident continuing the writing process once the writer leaves the center.

> **Tutor**: Awesome! Yeah, I love reverse outlines, too. I use them a lot. You can definitely apply them to future assignments as well. So, what are your next steps for this assignment?
>
> **Writer**: I'm going to use the reverse outline to review the last two paragraphs that we didn't have enough time to revise. Then I'm going to ask my professor to look at my paper again in her office hours.
>
> **Tutor**: That sounds like a great plan. Do you feel confident continuing the assignment once you leave the Writing Center?
>
> **Writer**: Yeah, definitely. I think I'll come back in the future, but I feel a lot better now. Thanks.

Receiving and Analyzing Feedback

Tutors should utilize feedback forms to receive feedback about their tutoring performance and to ensure the highest-quality service for their writers. A feedback form is a questionnaire that writers complete at the end of the session, and the form requires writers to answer questions about the performance of the tutor and the writer's satisfaction with the tutoring services. Feedback forms should be distributed at the end of every tutoring session, and writers should be given an opportunity to privately and anonymously complete the form.

Although tutors may feel hesitant about "bothering" writers with feedback forms at the end of every session, the completion of feedback forms is crucial for the growth and development of tutors. By the same token, it is critical to remind writers that tutoring is both a privilege and a partnership; tutors experience myriads of training to conduct sessions, and tutoring requires the writers to respect that training just as the tutors must respect the writer's commitment to supplemental instruction (tutoring).

Both the writer and tutor contribute to the growth of one another by offering and receiving feedback; once the tutor finds patterns in their feedback form responses, they can devise ways to apply the feedback offered by the writer and improve specific areas of their tutoring, which consequently benefits the writer in subsequent sessions.

1. Provide the feedback form to the writer.

> **Tutor**: I'm really happy to hear that our conversations helped you develop your writing skills. <u>I'm going to give you the feedback form that I mentioned. It's anonymous, and your honest feedback will help me grow as a tutor.</u> I'll let you fill it out privately. Please submit the form before you leave. Thank you so much for visiting the

Writing Center, and it was lovely to work with you today, Mitchell!

Writing Tutoring Feedback Form

Tutor name: _____

Course: _____

Please circle or highlight the choice that reflects your experience:

My tutor took the time to welcome me into the center and acquaint me with the structure of the tutoring process.
Disagree Somewhat Disagree Neutral Somewhat Agree Agree

My tutor helped me establish a meaningful and realistic agenda that aligned with my goals.
Disagree Somewhat Disagree Neutral Somewhat Agree Agree

My tutor asked me questions that engaged my critical thinking and introduced alternative avenues of thought.
Disagree Somewhat Disagree Neutral Somewhat Agree Agree

My tutor shared observations that furthered my understanding of effective communication and the writing process.
Disagree Somewhat Disagree Neutral Somewhat Agree Agree

My tutor respected my ideas and demonstrated enthusiasm for my writing.
Disagree Somewhat Disagree Neutral Somewhat Agree Agree

I came away with concrete tools and strategies to strengthen my writing beyond the individual assignment.
Disagree Somewhat Disagree Neutral Somewhat Agree Agree

Overall, I am satisfied with the tutoring session.
Disagree Somewhat Disagree Neutral Somewhat Agree Agree

Additional comments:

2. Analyze the feedback during free time in the center. Look for patterns among the feedback responses and begin focusing on the areas that need the most improvement.

Feedback Form Analysis Checklist:

"My tutor took the time to welcome me into the center and acquaint me with the tutoring process."

- ✓ Did the tutor offer their name and pronouns?
- ✓ Did the tutor ask for the writer's name and correctly pronounce it?
- ✓ Did the tutor utilize open body language?
- ✓ Did the tutor ask about the writer's personal well-being and academic experience before entering the tutoring conversation?
- ✓ Did the tutor inquire about the writer's familiarity with the tutoring services and provide an overview of the structure of the tutoring session?

"My tutor helped me establish a meaningful and realistic agenda that aligned with my goals."

- ✓ Did the tutor inquire about the writer's goals for the session?
- ✓ Did the tutor ask how the writer visualized the session aiding to accomplish the writer's goals?
- ✓ Did the tutor clarify the time restraints of the session and consider how the writer's goals could be accomplished in that time?
- ✓ Did the tutor inquire about the writer's next steps in the writing process?
- ✓ Did the tutor encourage the writer to return to the writing center to answer any questions that remained after the initial session?

**"My tutor asked me questions that stimu-
lated my critical thinking."**

- ✓ Did the tutor ask foundational
  questions to check understanding
  before asking critical questions?
- ✓ Did the tutor utilize a variety of interrogative words to form questions?
- ✓ Did the tutor ask questions that
  encourage the writer to consider
  alternative perspectives?
- ✓ Did the tutor ask questions that
  enabled the writer to respond
  with more detail than "yes" or
  "no"?
- ✓ Did the tutor provide enough
  "wait time" for the writer to sit
  and think about the questions
  asked by the tutor?
- ✓ Did the tutor provide follow-up
  questions to further expand the
  writer's responses to questions?

"My tutor shared observations that furthered my understanding of the writing process."

- ✓ Did the tutor share observations that answered questions asked by the writer?
- ✓ Did the tutor share observations that would aid the writer in accomplishing their specific goals?
- ✓ Did the tutor share observations that would allow the writer to better understand principles of strong academic writing?
- ✓ Did the tutor share their experience as a reader to provide an outside perspective for the writer?
- ✓ Did the tutor allow the writer to act as the "content expert" for the assignment so that the tutor could focus on guiding the writer's thought process instead of worrying about "knowing all the answers"?

"My tutor respected my ideas and demonstrated enthusiasm for my writing."

- ✓ Did the tutor ask the writer if the writer agreed or disagreed with feedback received from instructors or peers?
- ✓ Did the tutor demonstrate active listening skills?
- ✓ Did the tutor validate the writer's ideas and offer them writing strategies that would illuminate their ideas?
- ✓ Did the tutor allow the writer to make final decisions about edits or revisions?

"I came away with concrete tools and strategies to strengthen my writing beyond the individual assignment."

- ✓ Could the writer articulate concrete strategies that they learned in the session?
- ✓ Could the writer visualize how to apply the strategies to future assignments?
- ✓ Did the writer feel confident about independently continuing the assignment without feeling as though the presence of a tutor is necessary for the student to succeed?

Additional questions to ask when reflecting on appointments:

- ✓ What went will during my session with [writer's name]? What didn't?
- ✓ What types of questions prompted positive responses from the writer?
- ✓ What types of questions prompted negative responses from the writer?
- ✓ Did I follow the suggested anatomy of a writing tutoring session? If not, how did the exclusion of [specific strategy or step] affect the session? How would its inclusion have affected the session?
- ✓ When did the writer seem most engaged or talkative during the session?
- ✓ When did the writer seem least engaged or talkative during the session?

About the Author

Chloe has studied and received writing tutor training at both Clovis Community College and the University of California: Berkeley. During her tutoring career, she has presented at the Supplemental Instruction and Tutoring (SIT) Expo 2018 and 2019 about supporting returning students and digital tutoring prior to COVID-19. She is currently a Ph.D. student at the University of California, Davis, where she is researching the relationship between undergraduate writing center usage and undergraduate engagement with campus networks and resources.

Chloe first developed a passion for writing by spending most of her free time playing computer games as a young child, thus resulting in her frequent reading of quests in World of Warcraft and typing to fellow players and friends. This form of communication, based upon reading and writing, served as the foundation for many of

Chloe's early friendships. When she is not tutoring or studying English, Chloe is still enjoying her love for video games, or she is spending time with her pets.

References

Cer, Erkan. "The Instruction of Writing Strategies: The Effect of the Metacognitive Strategy on the Writing Skills of Pupils in Secondary Education." *SAGE Open*, Apr. 2019, doi:10.1177/2158244019842681.

Hedin, Laura R., and Greg Conderman. "Teaching Students to Comprehend Informational Text Through Rereading." *Reading Teacher*, vol. 63, no. 7, Apr. 2010, pp. 556–565. *Academic Search Complete*, doi:10.1598/RT.63.7.3.

"Higher Order Concerns (HOCs) and Lower Order Concerns (LOCs)." *Purdue Online Writing Lab*, 2021, https://owl.purdue.edu/owl/research_and_citation/mla_style/mla_formatting_and_style_guide/mla_works_cited_electronic_sources.html

Hogan, Tiffany P et al. "On the Importance of
Listening Comprehension." *International
Journal of Speech-Language Pathology*, vol. 16, 3,
2014: 199-207.
doi:10.3109/17549507.2014.904441

King, Alison. "From Sage on the Stage to Guide
on the Side." College Teaching, vol. 41, no.
1, 1993, pp. 30–35. *JSTOR*,
www.jstor.org/stable/27558571. Accessed
28 July 2021.

Liu, Keming. "Annotation as an Index to Critical
Writing." *Urban Education*, vol. 41, no. 2,
Mar. 2006, pp. 192–207. *Academic Search
Complete*, doi:10.1177/0042085905282261.

Meyer, Emily, and Louise Smith. "Promoting
Fluency I: Getting Started." *The Practical
Tutor*. Oxford University Press, 1987. pp.
43-66.

Payne, Jessica D et al. "Memory for Semantically Related and Unrelated Declarative Information: The Benefit of Sleep, The Cost of Wake." *PloS one* vol. 7, 3, 2012: e33079. doi:10.1371/journal.pone.0033079

"The Pomodoro Technique." *Francesco Cirillo, Cirillo Consulting GMBH*, Berlin, https://francescocirillo.com/pages/pomodoro-technique

Ritter, Simone M, and Ap Dijksterhuis. "Creativity—The Unconscious Foundations of the Incubation Period." *Frontiers in Human Neuroscience,* vol. 8, 15. 11 Apr. 2014, doi:10.3389/fnhum.2014.00215

Student Learning Center Writing Program. *Thesis Statements.* Spring 2020. *Google Docs* file.

Tofade, Toyin et al. "Best Practice Strategies for Effective Use of Questions as a Teaching

Tool." *American Journal of Pharmaceutical Education*, vol. 77, 7, 2013: 155.
doi:10.5688/ajpe777155